Learning About Landforms

Caves

Ellen Labrecque

Raintree is an imprint of Capstone Global Library Limited, a company incorporated in England and Wales having its registered office at 7 Pilgrim Street, London, EC4V 6LB – Registered company number: 6695582

www.raintreepublishers.co.uk
myorders@raintreepublishers.co.uk

Edited by Rebecca Rissman, Daniel Nunn and Catherine Veitch
Designed by Steve Mead
Picture research by Elizabeth Alexander
Production by Victoria Fitzgerald
Originated by Capstone Global Library Ltd
Printed and bound in China

ISBN 978 1 4062 7223 9 (hardback)
17 16 15 14 13
10 9 8 7 6 5 4 3 2 1

ISBN 978 1 4062 7229 1 (paperback)
18 17 16 15 14
10 9 8 7 6 5 4 3 2 1

British Library Cataloguing in Publication Data
A full catalogue record for this book is available from the British Library.

Acknowledgements
We would like to thank the following for permission to reproduce photographs: Alamy pp. 9 (© Clint Farlinger), 10 (© Galyna Andrushko), 11 (© David Kilpatrick), 19 (© Aurora Photos), 24 (© Tim Graham); Getty Images pp. 6 (Stephen Alvarez/National Geographic), 7 (Richard I'Anson/Lonely Planet Images), 8 (National Geographic Creative), 13 (Kevin Schafer/The Image Bank), 15 (Hauke Dressler/LOOK), 17 (Gareth Mccormack/Lonely Planet Images), 18 (Witold Skrypczak/Lonely Planet Images), 25 (Joel Sartore/National Geographic Creative), 26 (William Storage/Flickr), 27 (Reinhard Dirscherl/WaterFrame), 28 (Henn Photography/Cultura); © Jason Gulley p. 16; naturepl.com pp. 12 (© Photo Resource Hawaii), 29 (© Jack Dykinga); Shutterstock pp. 4 (© photobank.kiev.ua), 5 (© apiguide), 14 (© alexmcguffie), 20 (© Galyna Andrushko), 21 (© Dumitrescu Ciprian-Florin), 22 (Luis Javier Sandoval Alvarado), 23 (© Domen Lombergar).

Cover photograph of Grotte di Tufo sea caves reproduced with permission of Corbis (© Mimmo Jodice).

Every effort has been made to contact copyright holders of material reproduced in this book. Any omissions will be rectified in subsequent printings if notice is given to the publisher.

All the Internet addresses (URLs) given in this book were valid at the time of going to press. However, due to the dynamic nature of the Internet, some addresses may have changed, or sites may have changed or ceased to exist since publication. While the author and publisher regret any inconvenience this may cause readers, no responsibility for any such changes can be accepted by either the author or the publisher.

Contents

Some words are shown in bold, **like this**. You can find out what they mean by looking in the glossary.

What are landforms?

Look around when you are outside. You may notice grassy hills, rocky cliffs, valleys or caves. Earth is made of these natural landforms. This book is about caves.

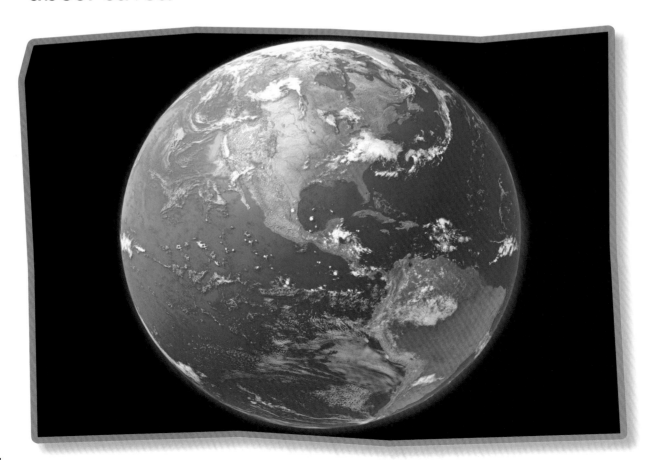

Earth is always changing. Earth's landforms are made in different ways over millions of years. For example, **erosion** wears down the land and creates valleys and **canyons**. Caves are made by erosion, too.

What are caves?

Caves are large, hollow areas inside a rock or under the ground. Caves can be difficult to find. Many times they are hidden away and only have a small opening.

Voronja Cave,
Abkhazia, Georgia

Caves take millions of years to take shape. The Jenolan Caves in the Blue Mountains of Australia are some of the world's oldest caves. They are 340 million years old. That is older than the dinosaurs!

Different types of caves

Caves can be so small that only a child could fit inside. Or they can be as big as 40 football pitches! Some have secret passages and water running through them. Other caves are just one big, dry room.

Mammoth Cave, Kentucky, United States of America (USA)

Jewel Cave,
South Dakota, USA

The four main types of caves are **solution** caves, **lava** caves, sea caves and **glacier** caves. Wind, water, air and even volcanoes make these caves into different shapes and sizes.

Solution caves

Solution caves are made when rainwater drips into tiny cracks in underground rock. The rocks are made of limestone. The limestone turns the rainwater into a solution.

Carlsbad Cave, New Mexico, USA

Aktun Chen Cenote Cave, Mexico

The dripping solution carves holes in the limestone rock. The holes become caves filled with water. After hundreds of years, the water drains and the cave dries out.

Lava caves

When a volcano **erupts, lava** flows down the mountainside and makes tunnels under the ground. The lava on top cools and hardens, but the lava underneath stays soft.

Kazumura Cave, Hawaii (USA)

Lava Beds National Monument,
California, USA

As the soft lava keeps travelling, it leaves a hole.
The hole becomes a lava cave. Lava caves are
also called lava tube caves.

Sea caves

Sea caves are made when the sea crashes against cliffs over a long time. Where the waves find a weak spot in the rock, such as a crack, part of the cliff gives way.

Fingal's Cave, Scotland

Blue Grotto Caves, Capri, Italy

Over time, more water seeps into the crack and makes the hole bigger. The water cracks the rock from the inside. Sand and rock carried by waves help to **erode** the rock more.

Glacier caves

Glacier caves are found on top of high mountains, and in cold places like the Arctic and Antarctica. Glacier caves are made when ice melts. The melting ice makes large holes inside glaciers.

Ngozumpa Glacier Caves, Nepal

Rhone Glacier Caves, Switzerland

As the holes from the melting ice grow bigger, they become glacier caves. Other types of caves, in places where temperatures go below freezing, have ice inside them too.

Wind and talus caves

Wind caves and **talus** caves are smaller caves. Wind caves are made from a soft rock called sandstone. Strong winds and water carve holes in the sandstone to make these caves.

Wind caves, Castle Rock State Park, California, USA

The Baths National Park,
British Virgin Islands

Talus caves are openings between **boulders** piled high on mountaintops. Many of these caves are small. Some, though, join up to make long paths under the boulders.

Cave features

Hidden in the darkness of caves, crazy rock shapes hang from the ceilings and rise up from the ground. Stalactites are icicle-shaped and are made when water and **minerals** drip from a cave's roof.

"Stalactite" has a "c" in it, which helps you to remember it grows from the ceiling.

"Stalagmite" has a "g" in it, which helps you to remember it grows up from the ground.

Stalagmites grow up from the floor. They usually grow from the water and minerals that drip off the end of stalactites. When they grow big enough, stalactites and stalagmites join to form columns.

Who lives in caves?

Troglobites are creatures that live in caves. Troglobites have become so used to cave life that they can't survive outside a cave.

This troglobite has lost its eyes, since it has lived in dark caves for so long.

olm salamander

Creatures that live in caves have very strong senses to help them feel their way around. In the dark, they don't need to camouflage themselves from animals that will attack. Many are totally white!

Fungi

Plants can't grow in caves, because plants need sunlight to live and there is no sunlight in caves. **Fungi** can grow in caves. They grow on the walls and floors. Fungi also grow on the droppings of animals that live in caves.

Guano, or bat droppings, play a big role in cave life. Creatures such as spiders eat the guano. Farmers also collect the guano and use it as **fertilizer** on their farms.

World's coolest caves

New caves are still being discovered today. The Difeng Dong Cave in China wasn't discovered until the 1990s. It has one of the world's largest cave entrances, which is more than 500 metres wide.

Underwater caves are hard to discover. The world's longest underwater caves are near the east coast of Mexico's Yucatan Peninsula. This group of caves is around 160 kilometres long.

Caves today

Caves are fascinating places to explore. But they can also be dangerous. You should never explore a cave without an expert. Caves are also **fragile**. When people visit caves too often, they can cause damage.

Cave creatures are also in danger because of **global warming**. These creatures need steady temperatures to stay alive. If caves get hotter and weather becomes wilder, they will die.

Glossary

boulder giant rock

canyon deep valley with steep sides

erode gradually wear away

erosion process where the earth is worn away by water, waves, wind or glaciers

erupt when hot ash and lava come out of a volcano

fertilizer substance added to soil to help plants grow

fragile easily broken or damaged

fungi living things like moulds, mushrooms or toadstools. Fungi live on dead or decaying matter.

glacier very large piece of ice

global warming gradual increase in Earth's temperature

lava hot, melted rock that comes out of a volcano

mineral material found in the ground or in water

solution mixture of two or more substances

talus sloping lump of rock fragments

troglobite creature that lives in a cave

Find out more

Books to read

Investigate Geography: Landforms, Jane Penrose
    (Heinemann Library, 2010)

Landform Adventures: Cave Crawlers,
    Pam Rosenberg (Raintree Publishers, 2012)

Look Inside a: Cave, Richard Spilsbury
    (Raintree Publishers, 2013)

Websites to visit

www.bbc.co.uk/nature/adaptations/troglobite
Check out some amazing cave creatures.

kids.nationalgeographic.com/kids
Type "caves" into the search box to find all kinds of information on caves.

www.worldatlas.com
Visit this great site to explore maps and landforms.

Index